VOLUME 2

## Developmental Reading Skills
*Decoding, Fluency & Comprehension*

# Kinder

# mini readers & workbook

THE MODERN MOM & BABY

Copyright © 2020 by The Modern Mom & Baby LLC

By purchasing this workbook, the buyer is permitted to reproduce worksheets and activities for classroom use only, but not for commercial resale. Please contact the publisher for permission to reproduce pages for an entire school or school district. With the exception of the above, no portion of this book may be reproduced—mechanically, electronically, or by any other means, including photocopying—without the written permission of the publisher.

Workbook series created & designed by Sukhjit Athwal

The Modern Mom & Baby Is a registered trademark

Printed in the United States of America

First printing Sept. 2020

# Introduction

Thank you for taking the first step in helping your child become a better reader!

Beginner readers need high-quality instruction and intensive support in order to learn essential reading skills. Data also suggests students need time to practice applying those skills.

Reading is made up of 4 major components:

*Phonics:* Scientific research has revealed that reading does not come naturally. The human brain is not designed to read. Children must be explicitly taught how to connect sounds with letters.

*Decoding:* Another big takeaway from decades of scientific research is that, while we use our eyes to read, the starting point for reading is sound. What a child must do to become a reader is to figure out how the words she hears and knows how to say connect to letters on the page.

*Fluency:* Sight words build speed and fluency when reading. Accuracy, speed, and fluency in reading increase reading comprehension. Children can also learn to decode other words by blending sounds.

*Comprehension:* With successful completion of each previous component, students will learn to understand what they are reading.

This workbook will help beginner readers transition into successful readers by learning sight words found specifically in this collection of 52 words that a child should learn with atomicity before entering Kindergarten.

As a successful reader, students will gain the confidence needed to continue reading, that in later life, help them in other subjects of study. The younger children start to read, the higher chance they have of gaining more vocabulary, alongside shortening the curve of being a struggling reader.

# Guided Instruction

*Please note: This workbook is to help beginner readers, and will prepare students in Kindergarten, to be reading at the end of a Kindergarten level, preparing them for 1st grade. If your child is having difficulty, refer to PRE-K Vol. 1.*

### There are three simple guidelines:

#1 Go at the pace of the student and acknowledge their efforts!

#2 Although it is tempting, please do not skip around pages, and follow the work as designed.

#3 Review often and as much as needed, in ways that work for the child *personally*.

Typically, students should take 10-15 minutes on the workbook a day, including reviewing and showing success on previous lessons, before moving to the next pages.

The workbook is curated into 5 types of lessons. Each lesson has a specific purpose and will be seen in multiple variations throughout the pages:

1. Sight Word Work—Prior to entering first grade, students should typically know roughly 92 sight words. These worksheets help the students focus on the word in multiple ways to make meaningful connections. It is helpful for the writing component, if a child uses a yellow highlighter or marker.

2. Point & Reads— After the completion of the specific Sight Word Work, students are challenged to use their skills by reading texts. These texts use easy to decode words and sight words that were learned in previous lessons. Children should review reads often to create fluency. (Pictures are not added to the stories, to help keep attention on just the reading and not allowing cues for the children or the ability to guess a word.) For a more advanced option, you can have you child draw a picture of what they read about or ask questions pertaining to the text.

3. Sight Word Benchmark— At the halfway point, you will come to the benchmark of sight words learned. This assessment should let you know what words the student it able to now identify and what words they may still need review in.

4. Assessment—There is a final assessment at the end of the workbook, that assesses the student on all 52 Dolch words. This can be taken twice on the same page, if additional practice or assessment is needed.

**Directions:** Cut out the sight words the child is working on and use as review. Only use the sight word cards that are currently being used in each lesson and story, in addition to any previous lessons. You can ask the child to show you a word, or ask them to tell you the words. Remember to be creative and make review fun in ways they enjoy playing. (Relay race, scavenger hunt, incorporate toys, pets, etc.) Be sure to add this as a quick daily routine, to maximize learning.

| | |
|---|---|
| am | at |
| with | too |
| be | on |
| who | he |

**Directions:** Cut out the sight words the child is working on and use as review. Only use the sight word cards that are currently being used in each lesson and story, in addition to any previous lessons. You can ask the child to show you a word, or ask them to tell you the words. Remember to be creative and make review fun in ways they enjoy playing. (Relay race, scavenger hunt, incorporate toys, pets, etc.) Be sure to add this as a quick daily routine, to maximize learning.

| | |
|---|---|
| do | out |
| want | into |
| new | white |
| four | black |

**Directions:** Cut out the sight words the child is working on and use as review. Only use the sight word cards that are currently being used in each lesson and story, in addition to any previous lessons. You can ask the child to show you a word, or ask them to tell you the words. Remember to be creative and make review fun in ways they enjoy playing. (Relay race, scavenger hunt, incorporate toys, pets, etc.) Be sure to add this as a quick daily routine, to maximize learning.

| | |
|---|---|
| like | ate |
| but | eat |
| did | no |
| so | have |

**Directions:** Cut out the sight words the child is working on and use as review. Only use the sight word cards that are currently being used in each lesson and story, in addition to any previous lessons. You can ask the child to show you a word, or ask them to tell you the words. Remember to be creative and make review fun in ways they enjoy playing. (Relay race, scavenger hunt, incorporate toys, pets, etc.) Be sure to add this as a quick daily routine, to maximize learning.

| | |
|---|---|
| please | brown |
| that | soon |
| will | under |
| now | there |

**Directions:** Cut out the sight words the child is working on and use as review. Only use the sight word cards that are currently being used in each lesson and story, in addition to any previous lessons. You can ask the child to show you a word, or ask them to tell you the words. Remember to be creative and make review fun in ways they enjoy playing. (Relay race, scavenger hunt, incorporate toys, pets, etc.) Be sure to add this as a quick daily routine, to maximize learning.

| | |
|---|---|
| all | they |
| are | get |
| say | came |
| our | well |

**Directions:** Cut out the sight words the child is working on and use as review. Only use the sight word cards that are currently being used in each lesson and story, in addition to any previous lessons. You can ask the child to show you a word, or ask them to tell you the words. Remember to be creative and make review fun in ways they enjoy playing. (Relay race, scavenger hunt, incorporate toys, pets, etc.) Be sure to add this as a quick daily routine, to maximize learning.

| | |
|---|---|
| was | went |
| must | this |
| ride | saw |
| yes | she |

**Directions:** Cut out the sight words the child is working on and use as review. Only use the sight word cards that are currently being used in each lesson and story, in addition to any previous lessons. You can ask the child to show you a word, or ask them to tell you the words. Remember to be creative and make review fun in ways they enjoy playing. (Relay race, scavenger hunt, incorporate toys, pets, etc.) Be sure to add this as a quick daily routine, to maximize learning.

| | |
|---|---|
| what | ran |
| pretty | good |
| | |
| | |

# am

**WRITE IT:**

**POINT & SAY THE WORD**

am   am   am   am

**TRACE & COPY THE SENTENCE**

I am in the big blue car.

# at

**WRITE IT:**

**POINT & SAY THE WORD**

at    at    at    at

**TRACE & COPY THE SENTENCE**

I am at school today.

WRITE IT:

# with

POINT & SAY THE WORD

with    with    with    with

TRACE & COPY THE SENTENCE

Do you want to come with me?

# too

**WRITE IT:**

## POINT & SAY THE WORD

too    too    too    too

● ● ● ●

## TRACE & COPY THE SENTENCE

I like apples too!

# Story 1

I am at the park with Bob. I am at the park with Jill too. I am at the park with Bob and Jill. I am not here with Tim.

# be

WRITE IT:

POINT & SAY THE WORD

be    be    be    be

TRACE & COPY THE SENTENCE

Will you be my friend?

# on

**WRITE IT:**

**POINT & SAY THE WORD**

on    on    on    on

**TRACE & COPY THE SENTENCE**

Sit on the mat to eat.

# who

**WRITE IT:**

**POINT & SAY THE WORD**

who  who  who  who

**TRACE & COPY THE SENTENCE**

Who was at the door?

# Story 2

Who is not here? Jim is on the way. He is not here. Who is here? Pam is here. Pam is here and Jim is not. Jim be on time when you are with me.

# he

WRITE IT:

POINT & SAY THE WORD

he    he    he    he

TRACE & COPY THE SENTENCE

He is taller than me.

# do

**WRITE IT:**

**POINT & SAY THE WORD**

do  do  do  do

**TRACE & COPY THE SENTENCE**

Do you like my cat?

## out

**WRITE IT:**

### POINT & SAY THE WORD

out   out   out   out

● ● ● ●

### TRACE & COPY THE SENTENCE

Do you want to go out?

# want

**WRITE IT:**

## POINT & SAY THE WORD

want · want · want

## TRACE & COPY THE SENTENCE

I want the red ball.

WRITE IT:

# into

POINT & SAY THE WORD

into　into　into　into

● ● ● ●

TRACE & COPY THE SENTENCE

Go into the room to play.

# Story 3

The sun is out and it is so hot. I want to go into the pool. Do you want to jump in with me? It will be a lot of fun! Now come on and jump in with me!

# new

WRITE IT:

POINT & SAY THE WORD

new   new   new   new

TRACE & COPY THE SENTENCE

Look at my new toy car.

WRITE IT:

# white

## POINT & SAY THE WORD

white    white    white

## TRACE & COPY THE SENTENCE

My hair is not white.

# four

WRITE IT:

## POINT & SAY THE WORD

four　four　four　four
●　　　●　　　●　　　●

## TRACE & COPY THE SENTENCE

I have four dogs at home.

# black

**WRITE IT:**

**POINT & SAY THE WORD**

black   black   black

**TRACE & COPY THE SENTENCE**

The fox is black.

# like

**WRITE IT:**

## POINT & SAY THE WORD

like　　like　　like　　like

● ● ● ●

## TRACE & COPY THE SENTENCE

I like my friends.

# Story 4

I can ride my new car. It is very fun. My new car is white. My car has four black dots. I like it a lot. I like my new white and black car with four black dots. It is fun!

# ate

**WRITE IT:**

## POINT & SAY THE WORD

ate　　ate　　ate　　ate

## TRACE & COPY THE SENTENCE

I ate all my food for lunch.

WRITE IT:

# but

POINT & SAY THE WORD

but     but     but     but

TRACE & COPY THE SENTENCE

I want to, but I can not go.

WRITE IT:

# eat

## POINT & SAY THE WORD

eat    eat    eat    eat

●　　●　　●　　●

## TRACE & COPY THE SENTENCE

I like to eat a lot of pizza.

# did

**WRITE IT:**

**POINT & SAY THE WORD**

did    did    did    did

**TRACE & COPY THE SENTENCE**

Did you hear that?

# Story 5

I bit one red apple. I bit into it, but I did not like it. So I ate a green apple. I ate the green one, but did not eat the red one. Do you like green or red?

# no

**WRITE IT:**

## POINT & SAY THE WORD

no　　no　　no　　no

## TRACE & COPY THE SENTENCE

Jim told Pat no.

# SO

**WRITE IT:**

## POINT & SAY THE WORD

so  so  so  so

## TRACE & COPY THE SENTENCE

So can you come over to play?

WRITE IT:

# have

POINT & SAY THE WORD

have    have    have

TRACE & COPY THE SENTENCE

*Have you seen my shoes?*

# please

**WRITE IT:**

## POINT & SAY THE WORD

please   please   please

## TRACE & COPY THE SENTENCE

May I have one please?

# Story 6

My mom said no dogs can come in my room. If it comes in my room, I have to say, "Dog please go out!" My dad said no cats can come in my room. So no pets can come in my room.

# Benchmark

Directions: Show the child each word from top to bottom on the left. If they are able to recite the word, place a checkmark in the box to the right.

| am | | white | |
|---|---|---|---|
| at | | four | |
| with | | black | |
| too | | like | |
| be | | ate | |
| on | | but | |
| who | | eat | |
| he | | did | |
| do | | no | |
| out | | so | |
| want | | have | |
| into | | please | |
| new | | | |

SCORE: ____/25

# brown

**WRITE IT:**

## POINT & SAY THE WORD

brown brown brown

● ● ●

## TRACE & COPY THE SENTENCE

The mud is brown.

# soon

**WRITE IT:**

## POINT & SAY THE WORD

soon    soon    Soon

## TRACE & COPY THE SENTENCE

Come see me soon.

# that

**WRITE IT:**

**POINT & SAY THE WORD**

that    that    that

**TRACE & COPY THE SENTENCE**

Did you do that?

# Story 7

Soon you will see my pet hen. It is brown with black spots. I want to put it in my bed with me, but my dad said no. My dad said that hens do not go in the bed.

WRITE IT:

# under

POINT & SAY THE WORD

under   under   under

TRACE & COPY THE SENTENCE

Did you look under the bed?

# will

**WRITE IT:**

## POINT & SAY THE WORD

will    will    will    will

## TRACE & COPY THE SENTENCE

Will you please come here?

# now

**WRITE IT:**

**POINT & SAY THE WORD**

now  now  now  now

**TRACE & COPY THE SENTENCE**

It is your turn to go now.

# there

**WRITE IT:**

**POINT & SAY THE WORD**

there    there    there

**TRACE & COPY THE SENTENCE**

The boy is over there resting.

# they

**WRITE IT:**

**POINT & SAY THE WORD**

they    they    they

**TRACE & COPY THE SENTENCE**

They went to play games.

# are

**WRITE IT:**

## POINT & SAY THE WORD

are    are    are    are

## TRACE & COPY THE SENTENCE

Are you okay?

**WRITE IT:**

# all

## POINT & SAY THE WORD

all   all   all   all

## TRACE & COPY THE SENTENCE

Can you all say hello?

# Story 8

Oh no! Where are my pigs? There they are! Oh my! They are under all of that mud! Pigs, why are you under all that mud? Now I will have to put you in the tub, to clean off all that mud.

# say

**WRITE IT:**

**POINT & SAY THE WORD**

say  say  say  say

**TRACE & COPY THE SENTENCE**

Will you say your name?

# get

WRITE IT:

POINT & SAY THE WORD

get   get   get   get

TRACE & COPY THE SENTENCE

Did you get your box?

# our

**WRITE IT:**

**POINT & SAY THE WORD**

our   our   our   our

**TRACE & COPY THE SENTENCE**

Our uncle is sick.

# Story 9

Did you get our card? If you did not get our card, can you tell me, so I can find it. I want you to get our card. It is from me to you. Tell me when you can.

# came

**WRITE IT:**

**POINT & SAY THE WORD**

came     came     came

**TRACE & COPY THE SENTENCE**

I came to say goodbye.

# well

**WRITE IT:**

## POINT & SAY THE WORD

well   well   well   well

## TRACE & COPY THE SENTENCE

Did you sleep well?

# went

**WRITE IT:**

**POINT & SAY THE WORD**

went  went  went

**TRACE & COPY THE SENTENCE**

I went to go drink water.

# Story 10

Pam came to the park and she did not feel well. Ron came to the park too. He did not feel well. So Pam went home and Ron went home too. Pam and Ron went home to get some rest in bed.

**WRITE IT:**

# must

**POINT & SAY THE WORD**

must    must    must

●       ●       ●

**TRACE & COPY THE SENTENCE**

You must go before it is dark.

# was

**WRITE IT:**

## POINT & SAY THE WORD

was    was    was    was

## TRACE & COPY THE SENTENCE

What color was the car?

# Story 11

I was with my new doll in here. She was my moms doll. She was white but now is blue. It is late now and she must go to bed. She must go to bed to get some good rest.

WRITE IT:

# ride

## POINT & SAY THE WORD

ride  ride  ride  ride

## TRACE & COPY THE SENTENCE

Do you need a ride?

WRITE IT:

# this

## POINT & SAY THE WORD

this　　this　　this　　this

## TRACE & COPY THE SENTENCE

This is your math book.

# yes

WRITE IT:

## POINT & SAY THE WORD

yes •     yes •     yes •     yes •

## TRACE & COPY THE SENTENCE

Yes, I am happy to see you!

# Story 12

This is my bike. I am so happy to have it. My sister said, "Do you like it?" And do you know what I said? I said yes! I like it a lot! I can not wait to ride my new bike.

# saw

**WRITE IT:**

**POINT & SAY THE WORD**

saw    saw    saw    saw

**TRACE & COPY THE SENTENCE**

I saw the bird fly into the nest.

# she

**WRITE IT:**

## POINT & SAY THE WORD

she    she    she    she

## TRACE & COPY THE SENTENCE

She is ten years old today.

# ran

**WRITE IT:**

**POINT & SAY THE WORD**

ran    ran    ran    ran

**TRACE & COPY THE SENTENCE**

He ran all the way home.

# pretty

**WRITE IT:**

**POINT & SAY THE WORD**

pretty  pretty  pretty

**TRACE & COPY THE SENTENCE**

That flower is very pretty.

# good

**WRITE IT:**

## POINT & SAY THE WORD

good　good　good

## TRACE & COPY THE SENTENCE

The ice cream was good.

WRITE IT:

# what

## POINT & SAY THE WORD

what        what        what

● ● ●

## TRACE & COPY THE SENTENCE

What did you say?

# Story 13

| She | saw | a | pretty | brown | fox. | The |

| pretty | brown | fox | ran | away. | It | ran |

| away | to | eat | good | food. | What | good |

| food | did | he | go | eat? | I | did |

| not | see! | I | did | not | see | what |

| good | food | the | fox | went | to | eat. |

# Assessment

Directions: Ask the child to recite the words in the list. Check off all words the child is able to successfully read.
*There is an option to take the test a second time for additional review.*

| | TEST 1 | TEST 2 |
|---|---|---|
| am | | |
| at | | |
| with | | |
| too | | |
| be | | |
| on | | |
| who | | |
| he | | |
| do | | |
| out | | |
| want | | |
| into | | |
| new | | |
| white | | |
| four | | |
| black | | |
| like | | |
| ate | | |
| but | | |
| eat | | |
| did | | |
| no | | |
| so | | |
| have | | |
| please | | |
| brown | | |

| | TEST 1 | TEST 2 |
|---|---|---|
| that | | |
| soon | | |
| will | | |
| under | | |
| now | | |
| there | | |
| all | | |
| they | | |
| are | | |
| get | | |
| say | | |
| came | | |
| our | | |
| well | | |
| was | | |
| went | | |
| must | | |
| this | | |
| ride | | |
| saw | | |
| yes | | |
| she | | |
| what | | |
| ran | | |
| pretty | | |
| good | | |

# CERTIFICATE of
# ACHIEVEMENT

awarded to: _____

in recognition of

# KINDER SIGHT WORD MASTERY

Date: _____

www.ingramcontent.com/pod-product-compliance
Lightning Source LLC
Chambersburg PA
CBHW041740160426
43200CB00003BA/32